STEVE PARISH · **TROPICAL NORTH QUEENSLAND** · AUSTRALIA FROM THE HEART

# Contents

## AUSTRALIA FROM THE HEART

*The north-eastern region of Queensland is one of Earth's most fortunate places. The long coastline is bordered by the blue-green Coral Sea, which nurtures the underwater wonderland of the Great Barrier Reef. Landward, magnificent beaches give way to fertile coastal plains, rising to the cloud-veiled heights of the Great Dividing Range with its fantastic rainforests and rushing rivers.*

*People come from all over the world to experience reef and rainforest, and the hospitality they are offered in Queensland's north-east is extraordinary. This is one of my favourite places, and putting this book together has allowed me to share some of the marvellous experiences I have enjoyed in this tropical paradise.*

*Steve Parish*

*Title page:* The Skyrail cable car gliding over the rainforest canopy.
*Preceding pages:* Rock formations, Cape Hillsborough National Park.
*Left:* Mingalli Falls, on the Waterfalls Circuit of the Atherton Tableland.
*Following pages:* Cairns, a tropical city standing between rainforest and reef.

The rainforest-covered heights of the Great Dividing Range form a backdrop to the green centre of Cairns, the major city of Queensland's north.

Dawn on the Cairns foreshore, a wonderful place to see waterbirds.

The Cairns Esplanade is a place for recreation and relaxation.

## CAIRNS, QUEEN OF THE NORTH

*Cairns International Airport was opened in 1984, and the city has become a favoured destination for world travellers and Australians visiting the Great Barrier Reef and the tropical rainforests. They discover a city that provides a base from which to take exciting journeys; a friendly city of magnificent gardens, great restaurants and a multicultural way of life.*

The Central Hotel and Spence Street at dusk, Cairns.

The illuminated façade of the Bolands Centre.

The entrance to Traders Row at the Pier Marketplace, a shopping plaza with style.

The Reef Hotel Casino, a place to play in the heart of Cairns.

When the sun sets, Cairns prepares for an evening of fun.

A coral cay is made up of coral sand and fragments, crowned with hardy vegetation and surrounded by a fringing reef.

Green Island, a coral cay 27 kilometres off Cairns, is a popular destination for day-trippers and holidaymakers.

The Great Barrier Reef is made up of numerous coral outcrops, each one inhabited by colourful life forms.

## CORAL IN THE SUN

*The Great Barrier Reef stretches down the coast of Queensland from Torres Strait to the Tropic of Capricorn. It is made up of nearly 3000 individual reefs, each composed of the limestone homes of countless tiny, soft-bodied coral polyps. As parts of a reef are broken away, waves deposit the debris in shoals that eventually rise above the surface. Seeds arrive by wind or water, plants grow, and seabirds arrive. The new coral cay has its own fringing reef, home to creatures of all sorts, sizes, shapes and colours.*

The Skyrail is an ideal way to see the rainforest. It journeys above the canopy from Caravonica Terminal to Kuranda and back.

## HIGH IN THE RAINFOREST

*The canopy of the rainforest is home to many amazing creatures. The Skyrail Rainforest Cableway carries viewers over 7.5 kilometres of tropical rainforest from Caravonica, near Cairns, to Kuranda. A more conventional view of the forest can be gained from the historic Kuranda Scenic Railway.*

The Red-eyed Tree-frog lives high in the rainforest canopy.

The Ulysses Butterfly is a splash of iridescent blue in the rainforest.

Australian King Parrots live on the rainforest fringes. This is a male.

*Top and above:* Scenes at the popular Kuranda Markets.

A train on the Kuranda Scenic Railway passes Stoney Creek Falls.

*Top:* Pied Imperial-Pigeons.    *Above:* Male Red Lacewing Butterfly.

# THE ATHERTON TABLELAND

*In the Cairns hinterland are the rainforests, lakes and lush farmlands of the beautiful Atherton Tableland. Nearly 900 metres above sea level, this scenic plateau enjoys a cool, crisp atmosphere. Abundant rainfall and rich soil weathered from the debris of long-extinct volcanos has fostered the growth of luxuriant rainforest. Much has been cleared for farms, but enough remains to frame some of Australia's loveliest waterfalls and a number of crystalline crater lakes, some of which are in the Wet Tropics World Heritage Area.*

*To the west of the Tableland are the historic mining towns of Herberton and Chillagoe.*

Millaa Millaa Falls on the Atherton Tableland.

Lumholtz's Tree-Kangaroo is a rare, leaf-eating rainforest dweller.

Sightseeing on beautiful Lake Barrine.

Lake Eacham lies in the crater of an extinct volcano.

The Atherton Tableland is renowned for its dairy farms, which supply north Queensland with milk products.

The Malanda Hotel is an old timber building that is famous for hospitality and good food.

Pleasure craft moored at Port Douglas, just north of Cairns.

The Low Isles, easily accessible from Port Douglas, consist of a coral cay and a mangrove flat. The lighthouse was built in 1878.

Pandanus trees stand sentinel over the coastline at Port Douglas.

## PORT DOUGLAS

*Once the port for the northern goldfields, Port Douglas has enjoyed a renaissance as a holiday resort. It offers world-class cuisine, shopping and accommodation, a fine golf course, and famous Sunday markets. More important for many visitors is its proximity to two of nature's masterpieces: the Great Barrier Reef and the tropical rainforest.*

A female Eclectus Parrot at the Port Douglas Rainforest Habitat.

## THE DAINTREE

*One of the greatest prizes for which environmental-
ists fought during the 1980s was the area known
as "the Daintree". It became an integral part of the
Wet Tropics World Heritage Area, listed in 1988.*

*This is the only place in Australia where the
rainforest drops right down to the coast,
overlooking fringing coral reefs. A striking feature
of the region is the rugged gorge that the Mossman
River carved through the forest as it flowed down
the Great Dividing Range. The sugar town of
Mossman, 75 kilometres north of Cairns, is a
jumping-off place for those visiting Daintree
National Park.*

The Cairns Birdwing, one of the spectacular rainforest butterflies.

Turbulent water rushes through Mossman Gorge in the south of Daintree National Park.

The Rose-crowned Fruit-Dove lives in the forest canopy.

The mouth of the Daintree River, which runs through the rainforests of Queensland's Wet Tropics World Heritage Area.

Saltwater Crocodiles are found in the Daintree and other north Queensland rivers. They will eat any prey they can catch and subdue.

Cape Tribulation, where the tropical rainforest runs right down to the aquamarine waters of the Great Barrier Reef.

Fan Palms are common in the Daintree–Cape Tribulation area.

The Southern Cassowary is found only in tropical rainforest.

Thrills are the order of the day when adventurers go whitewater rafting on the Tully River.

## SOUTH FROM CAIRNS

*Journeying south from Cairns, it is worth stopping at the sugar towns of Innisfail and Tully, both surrounded by rainforest that is listed as the Wet Tropics World Heritage Area. The Tully River rushes to the coast in a series of rapids, and a whitewater adventure down the river guarantees plenty of thrills.*

A modern clock tower contrasts with a stately colonial building in Innisfail.

Exploring the beach at Dunk Island, where lies one of the Great Barrier Reef's most beautiful resorts.

Time spent in peaceful contemplation is never wasted.

Catamarans ready for action, Dunk Island.

*Playground*

## DUNK ISLAND

*Dunk Island is one of the Family Group of eight islands, just offshore from Mission Beach. About three-quarters of Dunk is national park, and it offers a notable resort and good day-tripper's facilities. This is a marvellous place to walk, watch birds and other wildlife, play golf, swim or go on snorkelling and diving expeditions around the island or on cruises to the outer Reef.*

Lush rainforest grows on the inland side of Mission Beach.

Canoes, kayaks and catamarans are popular ways of exploring the sheltered waters around Mission Beach.

Hinchinbrook Island waters are paradise for sailors and anglers.

## HINCHINBROOK ISLAND

*Hinchinbrook Island rises from the sea off the town of Cardwell. An unspoiled wilderness and a national park, it rises to over one thousand metres at Mt Bowen. On the mainland side, the island is covered with rainforest. The seaward aspect features stunning sandy beaches.*

A family of backpackers on Hinchinbrook Island.

The fertile coastal plains of north-east Queensland, with their backdrop of cloud-topped mountains, are prime sugarcane-growing country.

Magnetic Island, with its lovely beaches and abundant wildlife, is only 8 kilometres offshore from Townsville.    *Following pages:* Townsville Marina overlooked by Castle Hill.

## TROPICAL TOWNSVILLE

*Third largest city in Queensland, Townsville acts as port for inland northern Queensland. It is a university city and a base for Australia's armed forces, with a popular hotel–casino and plenty of places to relax and dine. The Great Barrier Reef is some distance out to sea, but the Great Barrier Reef Wonderland, beside Townsville's Ross Creek, is a splendid aquarium that exhibits a spectacular living coral reef and a huge diversity of reef life.*

*The Town Common Environmental Park, a wetlands complex just north of the city, is home to fascinating waterbirds. For those interested in rainforest plants and palms, Townsville Botanic Gardens and the Palmetum offer a feast of native and exotic species.*

*Opposite:* A view over The Strand, Townsville.
*Above left:* Cycling along The Strand.
*Left:* Viewing an attraction at the Great Barrier Reef Wonderland.

Egrets, Magpie Geese, Brolgas and other wetlands birds can be seen in Townsville's Town Common Environmental Park.

A pair of Rainbow Lorikeets at their nest in a tree hollow.

## FEATHERED SPLENDOUR

*Bird lovers flock to the observation tower overlooking the wetlands of Townsville's Town Common. However, the city's streets and gardens are good places to look for such species as Rainbow Lorikeets and other colourful parrots that gather to strip flowering trees of their nectar.*

South of Townsville, the Great Barrier Reef lies further from the coast. However, its reefs and islands, such as Lady Musgrave Island, are just as stunning as those further north.

*Top:* Exploring the reef.   *Above:* An Orange-fin Anemonefish in its host anemone.

*The southern islands of the Great Barrier Reef are just as fascinating as the more northerly ones. The Whitsunday group are continental islands – mountain peaks cut off from the mainland in a past age by rising seas. Further south still are the coral cays of the Capricorn–Bunker group; these include Heron Island. All are fringed by intricate mazes of coral reefs that are home to multitudes of marine creatures.*

*Coral reef fishes range from huge groupers and enormous Manta Rays down to tiny creatures that resemble brilliantly coloured living jewels. None is more remarkable than the anemonefishes, which make themselves at home amongst the venomous tentacles of a sea anemone – the tentacles' sting is lethal to any other fish of comparable size.*

Sailing is one of the joys of a holiday in the Whitsunday group.

## THE WHITSUNDAY ISLANDS

*There are 74 islands in the Whitsunday group, which extends from the mainland town of Bowen in the north to Mackay in the south. These islands offer magnificent scenery, wonderful beaches and some of the world's finest sailing. "Bareboating", or hiring a craft to sail yourself, is a popular way to explore the islands.*

Hill Inlet on Whitsunday Island is part of a national park.

*Top and above:* Peaceful hideaways in the Whitsunday Islands.

Humpback Whales migrate to the warm waters of the Great Barrier Reef to breed.

The passages between islands in the Whitsundays are ideal for sailing, swimming, fishing and diving.

*Following pages:* A beach at Hamilton Island Resort.

Airlie Beach, departure point for the islands of the Whitsunday Group.

*Top and above:* Getting away from it all at Airlie Beach.

Cape Hillsborough National Park, 54 kilometres north of Mackay, offers a scenic rocky coastline and peaceful beaches.

The kangaroos that come to the beach at Cape Hillsborough share their recreational area with turtles and seabirds.

Eungella National Park protects an area of rainforest in the Clarke Range near Mackay. This rainforest has been isolated for many thousands of years.

Quiet watchers may spot a Platypus near Broken River Bridge, Eungella National Park.

## EUNGELLA NATIONAL PARK

*Eungella National Park, near Mackay, preserves an area of rainforest that is a nature lover's paradise. Creatures that live nowhere else may be seen here, and the elusive Platypus is often seen in the park's waterways. "Eungella" means "land of clouds", a fitting name for this mountainous reserve.*

A Sacred Kingfisher in Eungella National Park.

This Mackay landmark is typical of the bank buildings of former times.

The stately Charters Towers City Hall looks back to gold-mining opulence.

Wrought iron decorates the balcony of the Imperial Hotel in Ravenswood.

*Above right:* Colonial-style elegance in Rockhampton.

COLONIAL QUEENSLAND STYLE

*North Queensland buildings deal with the tropical climate in various ways: some keep heat at bay with solid masonry walls, others court coolness with cross ventilation and wide verandahs.*

VARIOUS REGIONAL TITLES AVAILABLE
WHY NOT VISIT OUR WEBSITE FOR FURTHER DETAILS?

*www.steveparish.com.au*

# *Australia from the Heart*

# INTERACTIVE CD-ROM

## FEATURES

- IBM and Mac compatible
- Over 150 images in each CD
- Nature video – 9 minutes of video introduced and filmed by Steve Parish
- Stereo soundtrack – high quality, original music
- Slide show – 8 minutes of breathtaking images set to music
- Desktop images – full screen in three standard sizes

- Screen saver – Steve's best Australian images
- E-greetings – e-mail or print
- Clip art – 24 Steve Parish images to share
- Storybook – with images, prose, music and poetry
- Photo tips – dozens of photography secrets from the master himself
- Steve's autobiography

*From an early age, Steve Parish has been driven by his undying passion for Australia to photograph every aspect of it, from its wild animals and plants to its many wild places. Then he began to turn his camera on Australians and their ways of life. This body of work forms one of Australia's most diverse photographic libraries. Over the years, these images of Australia have been used in thousands of publications, from cards, calendars and stationery to books – pictorial, reference, guide and children's. Steve has combined his considerable talents as a photographer, writer, poet and public speaker with his acute sense of needs in the marketplace to create a publishing company that today is recognised world wide.*

*Steve's primary goal is to turn the world on to nature, and, in pursuit of this lifelong objective, he has published a world-class range of children's books and learning aids. He sees our children as the decision makers of tomorrow and the guardians of our heritage.*

*Steve Parish*
PUBLISHING

Published by Steve Parish Publishing Pty Ltd

PO Box 1058, Archerfield, Queensland 4108 Australia

**www.steveparish.com.au**

© copyright Steve Parish Publishing Pty Ltd

ISBN 174021122 7

Photography: Steve Parish

Text: Pat Slater

Cover design: Audra Colless

Cover photo: Airlie Beach

Printed in Hong Kong by South China Printing Co. Ltd

Film by Inprint Pty Ltd, Australia

**Designed, edited and produced in Australia at the Steve Parish Publishing Studios**